THE GENERATION GAP

John Aylett

HODDER AND STOUGHTON
LONDON SYDNEY AUCKLAND TORONTO

Note to the reader

The words in heavy italics are explained in the glossary on page 32.

The Author's and Publishers' thanks are due to the following for permission to reproduce photographs:

t = top; b = bottom

BBC Enterprises: 24, 25b; BBC Hulton Picture Library: 15, 21; Barnaby's Picture Library: cover; The Bridgeman Art Library, private collection: 6; The British Library: 25t; Fleetway Publications: 22; The Home Office and *Daily Mirror*: 29t, 29b; Trustees of The Imperial War Museum: 20; Institute of Agricultural History and Musuem of English Rural Life: 19; The Mansell Collection: 8; Mary Evans Picture Library: 13t, 13b; Nestlé Milky Bar: 30; Punch Publications Ltd: 14; The Robert Opie Collection: 16; The Tate Gallery, London: 9; Topham Picture Library: 7t, 7b, 17, 28; John Twinning: 23; Vision International: 27

Artists: Roger Fereday; Tony Morris; Richard Scollins; Sara Silcock

Sources of quotations:
G. MacBeth, A *Child of war* (Cape, 1987): 21; The *Radio Times*, February 1983: 25; G. Sims, *How The Poor Live* (Garland, 1984): 9; J. Smith, *Edwardian Childhoods* (Routledge & Kegan Paul, 1981): 7, 9, 12, 13; Young and Willmott, *Family and Kinship in East London* (Routledge & Kegan Paul, 1957): 23

Every effort has been made to trace the copyright holders, but in some cases this has not been possible. The Publishers will be pleased to make good any omissions in future editions.

British Library Cataloguing in Publication Data

Aylett, John
The generation gap.
1. Great Britain. Families, 1900-1988
I. Title II. Series
306.8'5'0941

ISBN 0-340-48327-2

First published 1989

Published by Hodder and Stoughton Children's Books, a division of Hodder and Stoughton Ltd, Mill Road, Dunton Green, Sevenoaks, Kent TN13 2YJ

Photoset by Litho Link Ltd, Welshpool, Powys, Wales

Printed in Belgium by Proost International Book Production

Designed by Sally Boothroyd

CONTENTS

DIFFERENT GENERATIONS

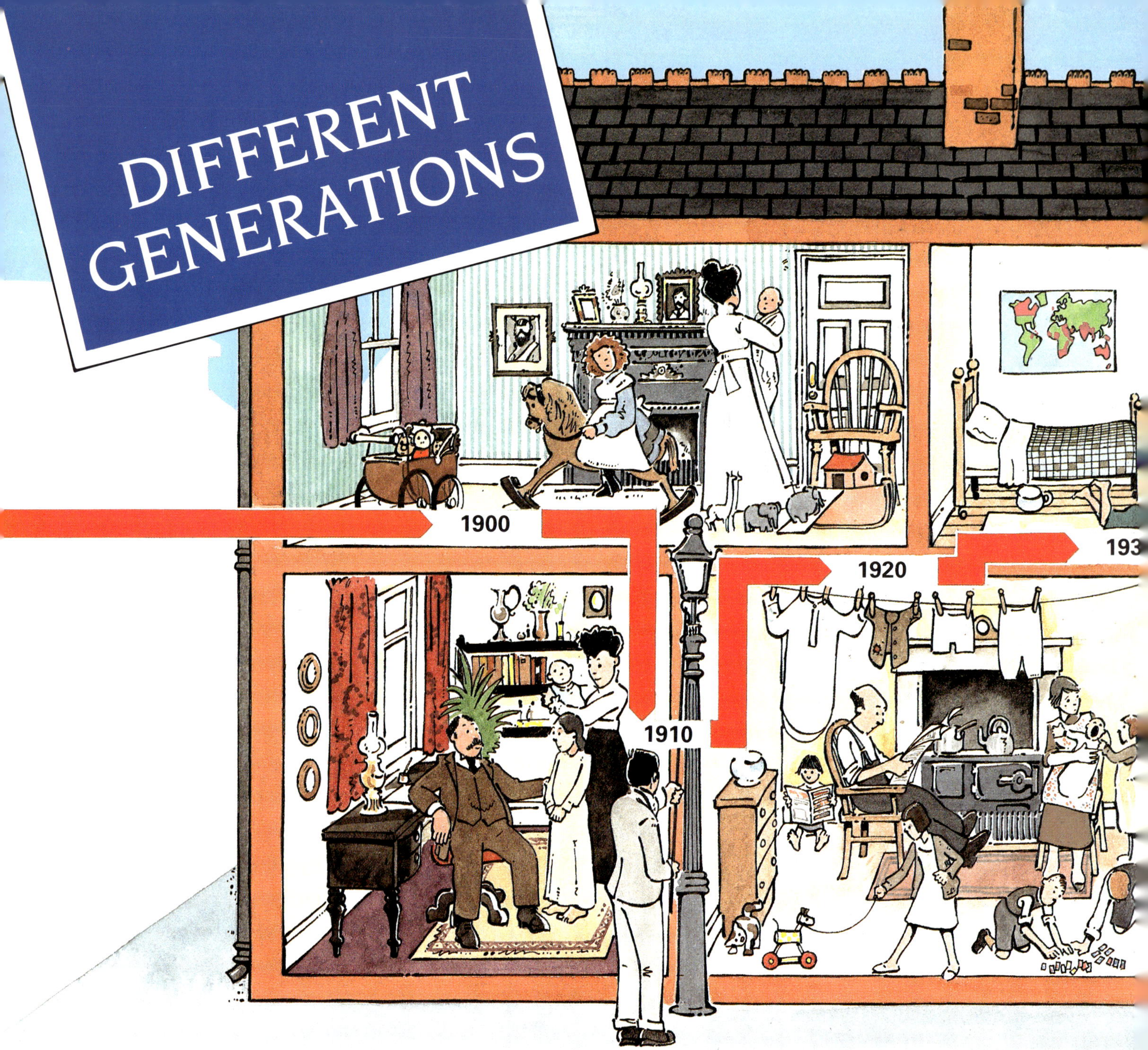

A generation is a group of people born at roughly the same time. A new generation begins about every thirty years. All the people born within that time belong to the same generation.

This is easier to understand if you think of your family: you belong to one generation, your parents belong to an older generation and your grandparents are from the generation before that. If your great-grandparents are alive, four generations of your family are still living.

This book is about the part played by older generations in young people's lives. Of course, the adults who have most effect are your parents. They bring

you up and control your life until you are old enough to go to school.

However, no two sets of parents are the same. Every family lives in a different way; it has different rules and ideas. For instance, some parents are religious while others are not. Some parents are strict but others are easy-going.

The time line above shows pictures of family life since 1901. These pictures cannot show everything about the families. They are like holiday snapshots which remind you of just a few things that happened.

WELL-OFF EDWARDIAN PARENTS

Edward VII was king from 1901 to 1910. These years are therefore known as the Edwardian period. Rich Edwardian parents thought that children should be kept out of adult life for as long as possible. Children, they believed, needed protection and strict discipline.

Rich children did not see much of their parents. Servants looked after them. The youngest children were looked after by a nurse. Slightly older children were under the control of a nanny. This was a woman who was paid to bring them up. When the boys were seven or eight, they went to boarding school.

MEALTIMES

Father saw the children at breakfast, then went off to work. He did not return until the evening. Many children did not even see their mother at lunch-time. Nurse fed the youngest in the nursery; another servant gave meals to the others.

◀ Rich people liked to have a family portrait. The girl on the left wears a short dress because she's not considered an adult.

Older relatives often lived with their children's families, like the grandmother in this advertisement. Would you have preferred to be in this family or the family on the left? ▶

When they were older, the children joined their parents for the evening meal. Their parents dressed specially for this meal, even if there were no guests. The children had to look smart, too. They could not just turn up in anything they felt like wearing. During the meal, they could only speak if their parents spoke to them first. Otherwise, they sat in silence and listened. Try doing this at a meal with your parents to see what it feels like.

A governess was a lady who taught children at home. This one is unhappy because she is about to leave. ▶

SEEING MOTHER AND FATHER

We only saw our parents after tea for about an hour. We put on clean pinafores. Our nanny said, 'Now, let me brush your hair and wash your hands and make you a nice little girl to go down and see mummy.' After we were about five we had lunch with our mother downstairs.

FATHER

I really knew father very little till I was grown-up. He was very busy. He used to come back rather tired in the evening about half past six. He used to say good evening to us and that was that. Saturday he might have gone shooting or out hunting. I didn't see him much. Sunday no – he probably slept all the afternoon on Sunday.

Do you think this boy's father played much part in his childhood?

. . . AND POOR EDWARDIAN PARENTS

The child that is not clean and neat,
With lots of toys and things to eat,
He is a naughty child, I'm sure . . .
Or else his dear papa is poor.

R L Stevenson

Poor Edwardian children usually saw more of their parents. After all, there were no servants to bring them up. Many children left school as soon as they were twelve to earn money for the family.

There were no family allowances then. Poor families could get some help from local charities. So many people were poor, though, that each family had to manage as best it could. Therefore, children needed to work.

Working or not, everyone had jobs to do around the house. Children were expected to help parents. If the father went *poaching*, one of his sons often went as well. The girls usually helped their mother with housework.

When it came to meals, the father often ate first. People thought he needed to keep his strength up to earn as much money as possible. Older children came next. In some families, little girls had least to eat. Some parents thought that boys were more important.

◀ Compare this family with the family on page 6. These parents are poor. How are their children's lives affected by this?

Poor mothers often worked part-time at home. The children helped after school. This family is making matchboxes. ▶

A NEW-BORN BABY

Few parents talked to their children as much as they do now. Mary Pink was 10½ when her sister was born. It was quite a shock to her:

My Father came in one morning and said, 'Go and see what your mother's got.' I heard a funny noise and said, 'What is that, a cat?' We didn't know things in those days, like they do now.

NEGLECT

Some parents did not look after their children well. One writer found a little girl of four keeping watch over a baby. Her father worked away from home; her mother went out and often came home drunk.

Think of that little child keeping guard on that dirty sack. She was left with orders 'not to move, or I'll kill yer'. Sitting there often till night, hungry, thirsty and tired.

Poor children quickly learned to take orders from other adults. They had to go out to work as soon as possible. Where do you think these girls are working? ▼

'Bless yer!' said a woman downstairs. 'I've known that young 'un sit there eight 'our at a stretch. I've seen her there of a mornin' when I've come up to see if I could git the rent. I've seen her there when I've come agin at night. Lor, that ain't nothing.'

FOOD FOR THE POOR, 1913

In the [poorer] household, only one kind of diet is possible, and that is the man's diet. The children have what is left over. As the man's food costs more, so the mother and children eat less.

BEING POOR

We felt cheated in some way, particularly when you didn't have things. Once I said, 'Can't have anything, we're poor.'

'Don't say that word here'.

How she brought that family up – I can't imagine how she ever did it. She told me once she had lived on cold water for three days so that she'd have just enough to keep the children going.

IN THE STREET

In 1901 there were more adults in a child's life than today. In villages, children helped out on the farms in summer. They got to know all the other families living in the village.

At dinner-time, they could sit in the blacksmith's warm forge and watch horses being shod. Or they could go to the carpenter's shop. He would be busy making anything from a window frame to a coffin. You probably know fewer adults outside your family.

Once in a while, a tradesman would come to the village, selling things such as fish. Town children saw a lot more of these strangers. Today, people rely more on shops and there are fewer callers.

Streets were a favourite playground for most children after school and during holidays. Streets were safer then because most vehicles were pulled by horses. They travelled much more slowly than modern cars and lorries.

THE CAT'S MEAT SELLER

He had a little cart with a lump of horsemeat on it. He cut it in slices and put it on wooden skewers. If you had a cat you went out and bought a halfpenny's worth of cat's meat. He was followed down the road by all the cats in the neighbourhood.

THE LAMPLIGHTER

Anything that happened out in the street was exciting to us. The one great joy of our lives was the lamplighter. He used to come down with a ladder, put it up against the lamp-post, then climb up it and pull on the light. We used to wait for the lamplighter. We waved to him. He was our pride and joy.

◀ Strangers were sometimes invited in for food and drink.

▲ Street people from early this century. Notice the muffin man, the lavender seller, the cat's meat man and the knife-grinder.

STRANGER AT THE DOOR

I remember a man knocking at the door and asking for old clothes. He had walked from Scotland where he'd got two children because he couldn't find work. Mother asked him to come in. She made him egg and cocoa and bread and ***dripping****. It was the first thing he'd had to eat that day.*

Father was away at work so Mother dare not give any of his clothes away. I can remember being so upset about this man. It made a deep impression on me.

There were several ways of lighting gas lamps. This lamplighter uses a long pole instead of a ladder. ▶

EDWARDIAN DISCIPLINE

Edwardian parents believed that children should do as they were told. In most homes, the father's word was law. It was often backed up by a cane or a belt. As a result, many children were frightened of their parents, especially of their father.

Most children obeyed their parents. All older people, children were taught, must be respected. Some young children were frightened of all adults.

Parents were very strict with girls. In 1901, rich girls did not go out on their own. One girls' magazine said, 'A young girl of eighteen should not be allowed out at all in the evening after *dusk*'. Many poorer parents were just as strict with their daughters.

SUNDAYS

Sunday was a special day in many homes. It meant wearing 'Sunday best' clothes all day – and perhaps a *clip* round the ear if you got them dirty! For Clifford Hills, Sunday afternoon meant Sunday School:

Mother would be waiting outside for us when we came out of Sunday School. We had to go for a walk with Mother, being very quiet all the time. Then we came back to tea, washed again, done our hair, off to church again, back home again, and so to bed. No playing on Sundays anywhere at any time.

OTHER ADULTS

We had particularly to respect the schoolmaster and the clergyman and the doctor. We had to raise our forefinger to him and say, 'Good morning, Sir.' Always 'Sir'. And we were taught, of course, never to be rude to people, or answer back.

PUNISHMENTS

Mother didn't hit us hard with the flat of her hand, but always had a cane up on the line – ha'penny cane. 'Course what we used to do was break the cane up or chuck it out. 'Where's the cane? Here y'are – go down the oil shop and get a ha'penny cane.' Never without a cane.

If a child was punished at school he or she was punished again at home, either by going to bed without supper or with a taste of dad's strap. It was a terrible disgrace for a child to get into trouble at school.

What happens to you if you get into trouble at school?

▲ This Victorian child is used to being beaten. Discipline was still very strict in Edwardian times.

◀ Going to church. A regular Sunday event for most people. The servants had to go too. Can you work out who they are?

A photograph of a well-off family. Who do you think was regarded as the most important member of the family in this picture? ▶

BETWEEN THE WARS

The 1920s and 1930s were years of terrible *poverty* for many people. By the middle of the 1920s, over 2 million people had no job. In the 1930s, it went up to over 3 million.

If the father had no job, life was hard. The government gave some money to unemployed people, but it was never enough. It meant cutting down on food. Many families lived mainly on bread and margarine.

As a result, many children suffered from diseases, such as *rickets*. This is caused by not having enough vitamin D; it stops bones growing properly. You had to pay to go into hospital, so many seriously ill children went without treatment. Their parents could not afford it.

GOING HUNGRY

These two passages show how parents went without food so that their children should not be too hungry. Can you think of a time when your parents have gone without something for your benefit?

Mrs J.'s husband has been out of work 14 weeks and there's five of them starving on 75p a week. Mrs J., a young woman of 26 had, as the neighbours said, 'gone away almost to a skeleton' through sheer starvation. Though she was nursing her baby, I found that all the food she had had yesterday was a cup of tea at breakfast-time, and tea and two slices of bread and butter at tea-time.

Hospital Patient (one of large family in poor district, given a glass of milk): "HOW FAR DOWN CAN I DRINK?"

◀ A cartoon of 1932. How can you tell that this child's family was poor?

A famous photo of the time. Father has no job. He spends his time hanging around on the street. The children join him. ▶

Father cooked sausages on the smoking fire, found a knife in the kitchen and cut the bread and spread it with margarine. We sat around on whatever we could find and ate a sausage each in our fingers. He managed to boil a pan of water and make tea in it. Mother drank much and ate little, refusing a sausage. Father finally ate, and only afterwards I realized that he had not had a sausage, and I felt a crushing sense of guilt about it.

Helen Forrester *Twopence to Cross the Mersey*

Nice people with nice manners
But got no money at all.
Their father keeps their mother,
Their mother keeps their brother
And when they're running short of cash
They borrow from each other.

Popular song

UNEMPLOYMENT IN 1937

Myself, wife and three children live on £1.46 a week. 105 individual meals each week must be provided out of 15½p. This means that we live mostly on tea and toast.

The youngest child has had ***pneumonia*** *three times since February of last year. She is now suffering from* ***bronchitis*** *and is probably developing* ***tuberculosis****. The oldest child was in hospital last month with* ***pneumonia****. It was out one week and has now gone back again.*

Why do you think the children were often ill?

The year is 1939. This man is unemployed. He and his family are eating boiled fish and dry bread. ▼

FAMILY RULES, 1918-1939

Families today have very different rules, even about simple things such as mealtimes. The same was true in the 1930s. Some parents were easy-going with their children. Others expected their children to behave just as they had before the war. Do your parents ever talk about rules when they were young?

I asked people what rules their families had as they grew up between the two world wars. These are some of their answers. As you read them, compare these rules with those in your family today.

MEALS

When father came in he didn't want us around. He was very strict. He never swore and he never drank. There were proper rules for meals. We weren't allowed to talk. We weren't allowed to drink any liquid with our food either. He said the food never did you so much good. I never now drink my tea until the end of a meal until it's cold.

You never left the table unless you were given permission. We children spoke to each other but not to our parents . . .

*If we even put our elbows on the table, a little **withe stick** came out and tapped us. We didn't do it again.*

MANNERS

There were a lot more 'please' and 'thank-you's' than there are now.

GOING VISITING . . .

We didn't speak. But that's how we were brought up. My father had his position to keep up. I think children like that. If they're shy, they like to know where they are.

You just kept quiet and spoke when you were spoken to. Grown-ups just tended to ignore you in those days. When you came, they would say, 'Hello' and 'How are you?' and usually, 'Have you been a good girl?' Then we would go somewhere else to play.

PLAYING TRUANT . . .

*My brother played truant several times. Then the **attendance officer** came to the house in the evening when dad was home. My brother had a thrashing!*

◀ Advertisements give a good idea of family life for the better-off. You could compare this with modern advertisements.

Many families were larger then than now. This might explain why children were often expected to be quiet at table. ▶

. . . AND JUST PLAYING

Boys were allowed to play in the streets but girls weren't allowed to.

GETTING PUNISHED

We got hit with a cane on the rear if we misbehaved. Once, I had to go and buy it from the local hardware shop. We usually got punished for things like riding on the backs of lorries and trams.

Mrs Livesey looks out of the window of her house in 1932. How can you tell whether this district was rich or poor? Notice the sores on the baby's face. ▶

A COUNTRY CHILDHOOD

Few country children were well-off in the years between the wars. However, their lives were often better than those of town children. My uncle was born in the little village of Binham in Norfolk in 1915. Life was not much different in thousands of other villages at the same time. As you read his story, see how many differences you can spot between his childhood and yours.

Respect was something we learnt at home. We had terrific respect for the older men in the village. Dozens of them had fought in World War I; others had taken part in strikes. They all had their tales to tell.

When I was 11 or 12, I helped with the harvest. I led the big horses while the men loaded the wagon with corn. If you behaved yourself and worked well, they treated you well. There was a respect between you and them. After all, you'd be out there in the fields from 6.30 in the morning till 7 at night with just a bottle of tea and some cold food. You saw the work they did.

Some people you had to show respect to, like the **squire** *and his family. You were taught that in school. I remember one Sunday I was walking along when I met the squire's wife. But I had my hand in my pocket so I didn't touch my cap to her.*

She called me back. 'Why didn't you take your hands out and salute me?' I replied that my hands were cold. But she told me off for that.

Another time I was getting apples or something from a tree when the squire's son came along on a horse. Again, I didn't touch my cap and he said, 'When you come down here, I'll whip you.' But I managed to drop down the other side of a hedge and get away.

▲ Everyone helped in the fields at harvest time. Why are fewer people needed now to do this work?

▲ Children spent hours in village shops and people rarely minded. Count the small shops near you today. Why are there so few these days?

◀ The village blacksmith. What other shops might there have been in the village? Why are blacksmiths now quite rare?

The village policeman was a different matter altogether. I remember one fellow who was a real tough guy. He wouldn't arrest people if he could help it; he gave them a good hiding. A policeman would clip anybody's ear in those days. Once he gave me a kick up the behind when I didn't move fast enough.

If you were in trouble, the policeman would come round to your house. If he came to mother's, she'd give me a wallop. Mother always had a cane.

After school, we'd often go into the shops in the village. Mr Massingham ran a shoe repairer's. When his back was turned, we used to pinch his nails. It was every boy's ambition to use them to put his initials in nails on the beam of the shop.

Everybody knew you by your first name and you knew everybody else. There were very close relationships in the village. It was a good way of life for a boy.

Why not talk to one of your uncles or aunts about when they were a child? They will probably enjoy telling you about it. They may even have photographs you could look at.

THE SECOND WORLD WAR

The second world war split up many families. At the start, thousands of children left the cities to go and live in the countryside. They were called *evacuees*. The government wanted to keep them safe from *air-raids* on the towns. This was the first time many children had lived away from home.

They went to stay with strangers who had offered to look after them. A few children never saw their parents again because their parents died in the war. Others saw them just from time to time until war was over. However, many returned home even during the war because they missed their parents – or their parents missed them.

Many fathers had joined the armed forces and were away from home. Some mothers relied more on their children than in the past. How could children who stayed at home help their mothers? Can you think of ways they could help, apart from doing jobs around the house?

LIVING WITH STRANGERS

By the time dad came to see us a second time we were in a terrible state. I was so determined he wouldn't get away, I waited outside the toilet door. As he walked out, I took hold of his trouser leg and there I stayed until he said, 'Obviously, I'll have to take them home. If we are going to be killed, I'm afraid we'll all have to go together.'

How did this girl feel about living with strangers?

◀ A government poster of the war advised mothers to send their children away from the cities. The 'ghost' behind them is an adult that every war-time child knew – the German leader, Adolf Hitler.

This little boy's mother has just been killed in an *air-raid*. ▶

▲ Air-raid shelters were another world for city children.

WHEN FATHER WAS KILLED

George MacBeth wrote about the day his father died. In those days, boys were expected to keep their feelings under control.

I remember hearing something I'd never heard before – the sound of my mother crying, somewhere in the distance. Then, a little later, someone came in and said that I had to be a brave boy from now on and look after my mother, because my father was dead.

I don't recall it as being a shock. It was too soon, and I was perhaps too young, to feel any sense of grief. I didn't cry. I thought it was important not to cry. Boys didn't cry. My father had died, and he was a hero, but that wasn't something to cry about.

What does he mean by saying, 'Boys didn't cry'?

AFTER THE WAR

A sign that children were thought important – they had their own exhibition. The 'Boys and Girls Exhibition' in London was a 50s treat for children. ▶

Eagle magazine was advertised as 'The magazine you're glad to have them read'. Dan Dare was a popular boys' hero; girls usually preferred film stars. ▼

In the 1950s, there were more children than in any previous generation. As soon as war was over, many couples had married and started a family. However, their families were usually smaller than in the past.

Families were generally better-off, too. Most parents could afford to give their children presents which they had never had when they were young. One 8-year-old was given a fridge as a birthday present! Do your parents ever buy you presents that they want?

Parents also wanted their children to be well-dressed at school. Many parents worried about what school friends and teachers thought of them.

At the same time, adults remembered the 1930s when jobs were hard to get. Children in the 1950s were often encouraged to think about the future and aim for a good, safe job. Girls were usually still expected to get married, even if they also went out to work.

DR SPOCK

Relationships between parents and children became more relaxed.

An American called Dr Benjamin Spock told parents that children needed love and attention. He also pointed out that a father's love was just as important as a mother's.

Before the war, bringing up children was mainly the mother's job. The father dealt out punishments. In the 1950s, many fathers played a bigger part in bringing up their children. What sort of jobs does your father do around the house? Look back at page 13. Do you think this man did jobs around the house?

A FATHER'S PUNISHMENTS

There certainly has been a change. I whack mine now, but not the beatings like we used to have. When I was a boy most of us feared our fathers more than we liked them.

CHILDREN COME FIRST

When I was a kid Dad always had the best of everything. Now it's the children who get the best of it. If there's one pork chop left, the kiddy gets it.

If you're going to put your children first, you can't spend your money on drinking and smoking.

◀ If mum went out to work, the children had to let themselves in when they came home from school. Newspapers called them 'latchkey kids' because they had their own front door key.

'AUNTIES AND UNCLES'

During the war, many children listened to adult programmes for the first time. But *Children's Hour* carried on, too. A favourite presenter was a man called Uncle Mac. (His real name was Derek McCulloch.) He used to end his broadcasts with the words, 'Good night children, everywhere'.

In the days before television, children only knew adults whom they actually met – apart from the stars of Saturday morning '*flicks*' at the cinema. However, there was one other group of adults who had a great influence on children in the 1950s. They were the people who presented *Children's Hour* on BBC radio.

The first children's radio programme was broadcast in 1922. It was an immediate success. The presenters were all called Aunty or Uncle so that children could feel they knew them.

After the war, BBC (British Broadcasting Corporation) television started up again. BBC TV did not broadcast between 6 and 7 pm. Screens went blank. The idea was to help parents get their children to bed without any fuss. Does this seem an early bedtime compared to your own?

However, Independent Television (ITV) began broadcasting in 1956 and it did not close down from 6 to 7 pm. So the BBC had to change and its programmes no longer stopped either. *Blue Peter* began in 1958 and a new group of adults influenced children's lives.

◀ *Picture Book* was one of the first television programmes for children. Muffin the Mule was the main character. Does anyone in your family remember him?

Blue Peter in the 1960s. ▶

Today, children's programmes start and end earlier than in the past. There are many programmes for very young children but fewer for older ones. Look in the television magazines and see what has happened to the children's hour between 5pm and 6pm. What sort of programmes are shown now?

'CHILDREN'S HOUR'

I can remember trying to hush the grown-ups. Without the earphones they could not join me in the new world, as I listened to Uncle Laurie, Aunty Ruby and Aunty Effie. Above all, there was Horace, the naughty boy who used forbidden words such as 'mucky'.

CHILDREN'S HOUR IN WALES

I remember the closing announcement of Children's Hour each night was in Welsh. The Aunty or Uncle would say, 'Nos da blant bach annwyl; cysgwch yn dawel', followed by the translation, 'Goodnight dear little children, sleep quietly.'

▲ This magazine was published in the early days of the BBC. It cost 2½p.

DOCTORS AND DENTISTS

One adult who turns up in every child's life sooner or later is the doctor. Have you ever been so sick that a doctor had to come to your home? Perhaps your mother phoned up the surgery, asking the doctor to come and visit.

Until 1948, many people only went to the doctor as a last resort. Visits to the doctor used to cost money; visits *from* the doctor cost even more. In villages, the vicar sometimes helped out.

BEFORE 1914

You put your best clothes on when you went to see the doctor. Doctors were very much gentlemen. You made the house ever so tidy if the doctor was coming. You changed your nightie and straightened the bed. The bedroom was tidied too.

NO DOCTOR

Our vicar was a father to the whole village. I had a boil and this was lanced by the vicar on the dining-table at the vicarage.

BETWEEN THE WARS

The doctor had far more time before the second world war. He would come in and sit at the table and have a bite to eat. He would take time to sit and talk. When my little brother had pneumonia, there wasn't time for an ambulance. So the doctor just picked him up and put him and Mum in his car and took them off to hospital.

THE DENTIST

Dentists were more frightening than doctors. People often only went when they had toothache.

BEFORE 1914

*There was only **cocaine**, no gas. He used to say, 'Just pull my coat if I'm hurting you.' But you were too petrified to do anything. You just opened your mouth and he yanked it out. You weren't taught to clean your teeth like you are nowadays. I don't remember toothpaste anyway. I remember trying to clean them with salt and water. Most people had a mouthful of rotten teeth.*

BETWEEN THE WARS

The school dentist used to come to the village hall. I remember once I had a tooth out and had to stay at home for 6 weeks afterwards. It had given me ear-ache. My mother created a fuss afterwards because they'd never asked her permission.

Are your school dental inspections like this? Why do you think they have changed?

▲ The doctor was often the first person in a town to buy a car.

◀ The dentist arrives! His horse-drawn wagon came on market day to get as many customers as possible. Where did he treat patients? What do you think the band was for?

Today, people do not have to pay to go to the doctor. ▶

KEEPING SAFE

Children early this century had much more freedom outside their home. Country children especially were allowed to wander freely down lanes and over fields. Today, there is more traffic on the roads and parents usually like to know where their children are.

Adults teach children not to accept lifts or sweets from strangers. Before 1914, parents rarely worried about anyone attacking their child. Teenage girls were often warned not to go out alone, but young children were usually given more freedom.

Some children suffered in their own home. There were cases of children being beaten or abused, especially by drunken parents. In some poorer homes, children were very badly treated. However, strangers were less of a problem. Anyway, in villages, strangers were few and far between. If any turned up, someone would probably go out and ask who they were and what they were doing there.

FREEDOM BEFORE 1914

It was perfectly safe in those days. I had a great friend who lived up on the moors, in an old farmhouse. It was over 12 kilometres away. I used to ride there on my pony. Nobody thought there was anything peculiar about it. I was told when I had to be home. It was perfectly safe, because there were practically no cars and they knew nobody would touch me.

Even in the 1950s, country children still enjoyed more freedom than most modern children do.

About 1½ million children disappear in America each year. This picture includes a 'Safely Home' game to teach children how to deal with difficult situations and a milk carton advertising missing children. ▶

Never go with a stranger

▲ Police used this photo to persuade children not to go with strangers. What mistake is the girl making in the picture?

A MANHUNT IN THE 1950s!

There was news on the radio that a criminal had escaped from a local prison. So my cousin and I decided to go out and look for him. My mother knew we were going for a bike ride – but she didn't know why! We couldn't have been more than 12 or 13. So off we set on our bikes to track him down. As it happened, we got within 2 kilometres of where he was hiding – but we didn't know that at the time.

Would your parents let you go off cycling if they knew an escaped prisoner might be nearby?

TOT KIDNAPPED

A three-year-old girl was recovering from a vicious attack last night after being kidnapped in the street. The toddler's attacker lured her away from a friend and into his van. He carried out an hour-long assault before dumping the sobbing tot outside a shop with money to buy sweets.

The *Sun*, 1986

What can be done to stop events like this from happening?

◀ This poster from the 1980s teaches children to beware of strangers.

IMPROVING CHILDREN'S LIVES

In so many ways, today's children have better lives than children of ninety years ago. In 1901, a child's future mainly depended on how well-off its parents were. *Governments* did not interfere with family life: they believed that it was up to parents to look after their children.

However, ideas changed during Edwardian times. The government became worried at the poor health of so many young people. Town children suffered from living in *slums*, where the air was *polluted*. Their parents often neglected them. Above all, they were underfed.

In 1906, school meals were started. The first town to introduce them was Bradford. Its children quickly put on weight – during term time. Bradford also organised school medical inspections. The rest of the country started them in 1907.

Most *politicians* now accepted that the country had to protect those who could not protect themselves. The government had already banned children from working at night. Children under 11 were not allowed to work at all.

However, the government did not really tackle the problem of poverty until 1946 when family allowances began. The government paid parents 25p a week for each child after the first one. (The money went further then than 25p would nowadays!) This is now called Child Benefit.

The start of the National Health Service in 1948 meant that all children could get free medical care when they needed it. Even today, there is no charge for children's prescriptions.

Politicians will continue to have an effect on your lives – and those of *your* children. What do you think life will be like for them in the *next* century?

▲ On the right, the 1987 'Milky Bar Kid', David King, aged 12. Left: his brother, dressed as a boy of 1937. Does anyone in your family remember being dressed like this?

HAS EVERYTHING IMPROVED?

Life was quiet and peaceful. We lived in hard times, but being children, we did not fully realise it. We were happy and always busy. My mother's motto was 'The devil finds mischief for idle hands to do.' There was no such thing as being bored as children – we never had time.

BOREDOM, 1987

Children are bored with their toys, their schools and their activities in general. They expect to be entertained. They lack the active enthusiasms of their elders.

A survey carried out by Nestlé in 1987.

▲ Today's youngster in a high-tech world. Is 'talking' to the computer replacing talking to adults? Is watching television replacing talking to children?

Mealtime in 1911 and mealtime in 1989. How many changes can you see? ▼

Golf Around the Channel Islands

Stuart Abraham

Les Mielles Golf & Country Club

LA MOYE GC JERSEY

Les Ormes

Royal Guernsey Golf Club

ROYAL JERSEY GOLF CLUB

1925 ST. CLEMENTS GOLF CLUB

St Pierre Park Golf Club Guernsey

WHEATLANDS

GOLF AROUND THE CHANNEL ISLANDS

Let me first say why I was inspired to produce this book. From a photographic point of view, the answer is clear. The scenic views on or from every one of the ten courses in the Channel islands are exceptional. Clubhouse, fairways, sand, trees and water. That's what most golfers around the world are used to and even to the least cynical player it can all look a bit artificial in spite of the man-made challenges and obstacles put in the way to prevent players hitting every green in regulation.

Channel Island courses are different. Water is a dramatic seascape; sand is a sweeping white beach; trees are part of a deep, verdant valley; fairways run along the natural contours of common land. Except for ponds, bunkers and special turf nothing else has been put there to disturb the eye. You therefore get the best, most, natural, uninhibited views of the islands from their courses.

Throw in some old granite farm buildings, Mediaeval castles, Napoleonic towers, Victorian fortresses, and ponds brimming with bird-life, gorseland and scrub then you are presented with a unique environment in which to play the game.

The photographs in this book were by and large shot in fine conditions or before the weather closed in during early autumn. But that's not always the case. Wind, rain, hail won't normally stop a golfer in this part of the world. A seven- iron on a hole last week can be a three-wood the next.Most of the time though the sunshine and light prevail.

I do have a passion for the game and come from a golfing family who spent many Sundays together on the Royal Jersey links. My grandmother ran Verona Stores, a short walk from the common, and won numerous competitions when she later moved to St. Clements.

On trips abroad in recent years, when not taking pictures professionally, I try and get a game if time allows. I've played in Finland on tundra grass, in India with cobras in the bushes, in South Africa with giraffes in the rough, at an exclusive club in southern Japan with a lady caddy dressed like a bee-keeper and in Germany on a course attached to a nun's convent. To cap it all, in 2001, I was a guest player in the President's Cup at Moscow Country Club and had a beer with six ambassadors afterwards.

Jersey golfers might not have ventured as far as Guernsey or Alderney and vice versa. Further afield there are thousands of golfers and non-golfers who may never have heard of the Channel Islands. To avoid argument, I should like to end by pointing out that this book is not laid out in any order of merit other than the fact the largest island appears first because it has more courses. I hope other golfers are inspired to come and play in these special locations and enjoy the hospitality that the Channel Islands are famous for.

ALDERNEY

LA GRANDE MARE

LES MIELLES

LA MOYE

LES ORMES

ROYAL GUERNSEY

ROYAL JERSEY

ST. CLEMENTS

ST PIERRE PARK

WHEATLANDS

JERSEY • GUERNSEY • ALDERNEY

Golf Around The Channel Islands is published by Rocco Publishing, P.O. Box 735, St. Helier, Jersey, JE4 0QN.
Tel: (01534) 484716
Mobile: 07797 713988
E-mail: sales@jerseyphotos.co.uk

Design: Eddie McGrath, Untitled Folder Limited (01534) 730325

British Library Cataloguing in Publication Data:
Abraham, Stuart
Golf Around the Channel Islands
ISBN 0-9517252-1-1

"The photographs and descriptions give a true and professional reflection of the terrific variety of golf available in these small islands".

Harry Vardon was always my hero when I grew up at the Royal Jersey. I did not play any other golf course until I was 15 years old. Happily, I have now played all the Channel Island courses among the thousands I have on my travels around the world.

I am delighted to be associated with Stuart's contribution to Channel Island golf.

The photographs and descriptions give a true and professional reflection of the terrific variety of golf available in these small islands. We now have three golf courses which have been in existence for over a century so we have a vast history of golf here.

The introduction of Les Mielles and all the newer courses have become essential to these islands due to the demands of islanders and visitors alike.

When flying back after competing abroad, I always look down from the plane to see these familiar courses in their marvellous settings.

My own hopes are for the future of golf in Jersey and the other islands. I do as much as I can to encourage juniors. Great efforts are being made, largely due to the Harry Vardon Trust fund, to introduce golf to over 400 school children during the next two years. With support like this, the future of golf in these small islands is guaranteed.

Tommy Horton, M.B.E.

LA MOYE GOLF CLUB

The youngest of the old courses in the Channel Islands, La Moye celebrated its centenary in 2002 with a full programme of events and has been given pride of place at the beginning of this book in honour of the occasion.

Secretary, Chris Greetham, kindly allowed me

photographic access and it is fitting that the two main front cover shots were taken within minutes of one another as the setting sun turned the rolling 17th fairway a golden green and the warmth of the sky presented a picture of the other islands across St. Ouen's Bay with the 15th pin in the foreground.

Many hundreds of visitors, amateurs and professionals alike, have played this well-maintained course over the years.Its condition never falters even during the driest summers (when they appear) and it has hosted many major championships including the Jersey Open until 1995 and subsequently the Jersey Seniors Masters.

It was at the latter event in the Year 2000 that Neil Coles at the tender age of 65 made history by becoming the first golfer to win a professional event in six different decades.

Indeed,history and tradition has played a big part in the development of the La Moye club.

Whereas Harry Vardon's name is closely associated with the Royal Jersey, it was his schoolmaster, George Boomer (whose pupils also included Ted Ray and his own sons Aubrey and Percy) who laid out the western course using a hand lawnmower and empty fruit cans for holes. At one time the course went right down to beach level.

The full story of La Moye entitled " The First One Hundred Years" has been carefully documented in a book by Peter Firth.

Among the many stories within the pages the author tells how five times Open champion, James Braid, probably one of the finest golf architects of all time, braved his fear of sea travel to come to Jersey in the 1930s to re-design the course, but the records of his work along with the clubhouse and many of the greens and fairways were destroyed by occupying forces during the war years.

La Moye has changed quite considerably since those days but "it continues to offer a challenge to golfers of every ability in a setting few other courses can match."

La Moye

LA MOYE GOLF CLUB

JERSEY

THE ROYAL JERSEY GOLF CLUB

Much has been done in recent years to promote the Vardon name and his association with the links at Grouville. An exhibition match in 1984 between Jack Nicklaus, Hale Irwin, Brian Barnes and Tommy Horton, got the ball rolling when the Harry Vardon Trust was established.

Later, the unveiling of a lifesize bronze statue of "The Golf King" at the entrance and the presentation of a miniature to Tiger Woods have all had great effect. Harry Vardon won a record six Open titles, but his victory in the US Open Championship in 1900 certainly went to show the disproportionate impact Jersey had on the golfing world at the time.

It took another 50 years before another Englishman lifted the US Crown. Tony Jacklin was a resident of the Island for a time.

Another resident, Tommy Horton, the Club's former professional and Ryder Cup player , has added to Jersey's rich golfing legacy by securing a record five Order of Merit titles in the European Seniors tour.The Vardon Trophy was awarded for first time in 1937 and is now presented to the touring player with the season's lowest adjusted scoring average. Tiger Woods has won it for three consecutive years.

The son of a gardener, Harry Vardon, was born in 1870, and honed his skill by hitting a large marble around his own golf holes with handmade clubs. He caddied for wealthy golfers playing the game on the new course near his home and developed his style by watching them. The overlapping or "Vardon Grip" he popularised is used by 70% of players today.

His brother Tom was the first of all the Jersey players, which included Ted Ray, the only other Jerseyman to win the British Open, to take up a professional post in England. Harry left Jersey to take up a similar post in 1890 and won his first Open title in 1896.

The Club was established by a group of enthusiasts and officers of the militia based at Fort Henry in the same year as Vardon's birth and the word Royal was added by Queen's warrant the following year.The layout of the course in some way indicates the scarcity of land on the island and its compact nature has changed little since Vardon's day. The sweep of the Royal Bay of Grouville, a particular favourite of Queen Victoria, always leads the eye towards Mont Orgueil Castle and there is no better view than the one from the 18th green.

THE ROYAL JERSEY GOLF CLUB

LES MIELLES GOLF CLUB

It was nearly forty years ago that cattle breeder Jack A'Court sold up and established a golf driving range, only the second of its type in the U.K. at the time, on part of his land in St. Ouen's Bay.

Ten years later an application was made to establish a nine-hole course Par 3 course and this was subsequently extended to 12 holes in 1986 by the founder's grandson, Jon Le Brun, who took over the running of the centre. By 1990, with the game flourishing in the Island, there was strong demand for the creation of a third 18-hole course.

Adjoining land was acquired to complete the project which would be an American-style course with numerous water hazards, dwarf rye fairways and bent grass greens, the first of its type in the Channel Islands. With the addition of a covered driving range, mini-golf, putting green, practice bunkers, chipping areas,restaurant, club house and pro shop, the Les Mielles Golf & Country Club is now well-established as a quality "pay and play" course. It attracts many visiting players and hosted its most prestigious tournament to date in 2002 with the staging of the Jersey PGA Players Championship.

What makes Les Mielles unusual in comparison to many courses is the diversity of bird-life found on the course at all times of the year but particularly through the colder months when migrating species from northern climes arrive to winter there. The reedbeds and nearby tideline,dunes, scrub and open grassland are breeding grounds for many other types of resident birds including Oystercatcher, Coot, Moorhen, Bunting and Warbler.

The course is continuously changing and being improved with new tee boxes, bunker placements and re-arrangement of the water hazards. The Par 34 front nine or north course is very testing for mid- to high-handicappers particularly in high winds as water comes into play on every single hole. The Par 36 back nine allows players to open up a little more but still calls for accuracy, distance judgement and proper course management.

LES MIELLES GOLF CLUB

JERSEY

WHEATLANDS

WHEATLANDS GOLF CLUB

A bit of bulldog spirit and stubborn determination not to give up resulted in developer, Nick Le Couteur, getting the necessary permission to construct his 9-hole inland "executive" course on the slopes bordering St. Peter's Valley even though a full sitting of Jersey's government, The States, was required before work could proceed.

Parish resident, Ian Woosnam, accepted the invitation some three years later to open Wheatlands and since then it has matured into a course of considerable merit, providing even the best players with a stern test of the game thanks to its clover-shaped design. Rather than being just up and down, the lay out means that at least two tees always face the prevailing wind.

French senior, Alain Rougeot, described Wheatlands as "one of the most beautiful courses I have seen in my travels around the world". No doubt he was inspired by surroundings of mature woodland,a natural habitat of barn owls, kestrels and families of red squirrels.

The later addition of twin tees has resulted in more failure than success in cracking par over 18 holes and, in fact, only two professionals have achieved it but no amateurs to date. There's one hole that has destroyed more

cards that can be counted. The awesome slopes of the aptly named, Heartbreak Hill, have been known to make many a grown man weep.

Perhaps the hardest Par 3 course in the Channel Islands, Wheatlands is also an ideal place to stay and play at the intimate, well run hotel on site, and has certainly helped golf tourism to Jersey.

WHEATLANDS GOLF CLUB

JERSEY

LES ORMES GOLF CLUB

Awesome views are available from many of the fairways and greens at Les Ormes which has been built on a plateau above the protected dune system at the southern end of St. Ouen's Bay.

This was formerly a campsite, but the windswept ridge is far better suited to a golf course than nights under canvas as the burgeoning membership of this fast expanding leisure complex would agree. The facilities, which also include some of the best indoor tennis available, are under the administration of a trust called the Bosdet Foundation.

If permission were granted, then there is a chance at some time in the future that this attractive nine-holer might become Jersey's fourth 18-hole course. That would almost link them up with La Moye a little further to the south.

For the time being though, the nine holes must be played twice (from the same tees) for a full card but with the changeable wind conditions that often prevail 250 feet above sea level that can be a challenge in itself.

The greens on three of the longest Par 4s are perched on the edge of the dunes and, with a squall coming off the Atlantic, putting a good card together can prove tough if you have to drive into the teeth of a gale. Of the shorter holes, the 4th has been described as one of the finest Par 3s in the Channel Islands. It is protected by a small valley, new bunkers to the front and trees on both sides.

The 9th too is an excellent little hole as you must fire your shot over a deep ravine, full of undergrowth, that has gobbled up more balls than you'd care to count. The addition of a surplus of pot bunkers has turned Les Ormes into a difficult test of golf and, with its excellent training facilities, is a good place to learn the game.

LES ORMES GOLF CLUB

JERSEY

ST. CLEMENTS GOLF CLUB

For a course to be called a battlezone might seem a rather unfair description bearing in mind that golf is meant to be a recreational activity.

Over the last ten years or so, substantial improvements have been made to Jersey's only 9-hole "urban" course at St. Clements Recreation Grounds, but before that it had a reputation for being a rather dangerous place to play the game.

Nobody could ignore the signs that warned: " Beware of Flying Golf Balls" because of the number of crossover holes.

The 4th, 5th, 6th, 8th and 9th all had potential problems in this respect, let alone for the cyclists and walkers who risked being hit by an errant bounce or drive when they used the road on the north side.

Land limitations did not deter the group of enthusiasts including Carlisle le Gallais, Edward Mossop and Jack Willcox, who were among the key people involved in establishing the course which celebrated its 75th anniversary in the Year 2000. Many golfers have since learned to play the game there, including Trevor Gray, one of the Channel

Islands' most successful amateurs.

St. Clements is run on a non-profit making basis so nearly all monies, except for a small dividend, is ploughed back into the course. The condition has improved quite dramatically over the past decade, the most important step being the lease of a field at the eastern end allowing the course to be re-modelled and crossing fairways removed.

There has also been a large tree-planting programme together with the purchase of new machinery and sprinklers.

Drainage problems have been addressed and most recently the old office has been replaced with a timber-framed management centre.

From humble beginnings, St Clements has responded to the growth in interest in the game and now it would be difficult to find anyone who has negative comments to make about the course.

ST. CLEMENTS GOLF CLUB

JERSEY

Royal Guernsey Golf Club

ROYAL GUERNSEY GOLF CLUB

The history of the Royal Guernsey Golf Club goes back such a long way that four different courses have been used since it started in 1890.

Old Tom Morris, one of the founding fathers of the Royal & Ancient at St. Andrews and usually referred to as the original professional golfer, was invited to redesign the first course. He was so pleased with the L'Ancresse links that on walking to the top of the Cromlech and casting his eye over the lie of the land said: "It is just pairfect and could na be better."

The description has changed little since Horace Hutchinson wrote:

"You find yourself looking out over the most glorious seascape which extends to three-quarters of your horizon. The cliffs are bold and rugged and rocks in the sea relieve its blue and break into foam.The golf course sweeps down from you and then away up on your right hand, in a fine natural curve of beauty."

The Club received its Royal Warrant in June 1891 and the first inter-island match was played in 1895. A professional match between the famous Ted Ray and T. Boutell took place in August 1899. A number of improvements were made and the lay out revised twice more before WW2. Unfortunately, few of the old records survived the German occupation when fairways were destroyed and guns sited on the greens. The course was fully restored to a design by Mackenzie Ross and in use by the beginning of 1949.

Today, the common is a popular open space attracting a fair amount of animal and human traffic so golfers beware. Balls landing in hoof marks from cattle which are tethered around get a free drop. A similar local rule also applies to a ball coming to rest on or near dung, although the origin is not specified on the course card.

Dolmens, Martello Towers, German Bunkers and two roads near the 8th are all deemed integral parts of this testing course that climbs and drops across Guernsey's largest heath.

ROYAL GUERNSEY GOLF CLUB

GUERNSEY

LA GRANDE MARE GOLF CLUB

LA GRANDE MARE GOLF CLUB

If your idea of a golf course is one that has hills and valleys, rolling fairways, low tee boxes and high greens then La Grande Mare does not fit the bill.

From the coast road at Vazon Bay, its looks fairly flat and featureless but venture onto the course and you get a completely different picture of this 110 acre stretch of parkland.

Designed by Fred Hawtree and Sons, who are highly respected golf architects, La Grande Mare has matured dramatically since it opened in 1994. A quick look at the card will give the initial impression that it is short and easy to master but it is a deceptively difficult course.

The streams crossing the course are unseen; the main water hazards are quite significant in size giving the greens great protection, and come into play on all but 3 of the holes. The lines of growing shrubs and trees call for accuracy and good ball placement. The greens are smooth and well kept and the far, double greens are large enough to leave you with a putt of over 45 yards.

The most challenging Par 3 hole is the 17th, 266 yards over water. The other fact is that you are right by the sea, even though the course is built on a base of clay and peat, and there is normally wind from some direction to contend with.

As one reviewer put it: "The course features several short, but challenging, opening holes followed by a nightmare four hole 'Amen Corner' and a very challenging trip home amongst watery doglegs"

All in all, this course continues to evolve and needs to be played more than once to be appreciated. La Grande Mare is open to non-members and visitors can stay in the family-run hotel or one the apartments on site.

La Grande Mare

LA GRANDE MARE GOLF CLUB

GUERNSEY

ST PIERRE PARK GOLF CLUB

This challenging little Par 3 course is situated to the west of St. Peter Port within the stylish and peaceful preserve of Guernsey's most luxurious hotel.

Designed by Tony Jacklin, undulating parkland, formerly a large cider orchard, was used to create the course. Good alignment, strategy and skill to hit straight, accurate shots with mid- and short -range irons will keep most players out of trouble.

A full set is not needed here but one's short game should be sharp as there is an abundance of water placed to catch the unwary and this combined with land sloping away from the greens means that to have a good round you need to be on the green or very close to it other wise the hoped for 3 can turn into a 5 or 6, sometimes worse.

The most club you'll need is a three iron when the wind is blowing, otherwise or four or higher will suffice. On certain holes, two tee boxes are positioned to give a different approach to the green, adding variety and interest to this picturesque course.

The hotel is an important conference and meetings venue so the course gets plenty of corporate use both casually and competitively.

St Pierre Park

ST PIERRE PARK GOLF CLUB

GUERNSEY

ALDERNEY GOLF CLUB

If golf clubs around the world were given a rating for friendliness and warm welcomes then Alderney would come high on the list. This tricky, undulating course with sea on all sides,offers great views of Braye Harbour and beyond from its high tees and greens on one side and the coast of France, only eight miles away, from the other.

Designed by Frank Pennink, with new tees its nine holes double to a 5006 yard Par 64, which was only beaten for the first time in competition during 2001 by former resident professional, Peter Cunningham, who went round one under.

In spite of the impression that the course has been in existence for quite some time, probably because it blends so naturally into the landscape, play only started in 1970. The course was opened by Guernsey's Lieut.-Governor of the day who played the inaugural round with a local character who had hit the bottle beforehand. The story goes that this chap keeled over in the mud as he tried to tee off on the third. The Governor declared that they should carry on as a three-ball. Some time later the Governor returned to Alderney on another visit and spotted the chap in the clubhouse and promptly said: "Hello, nice to see you again" to which he received the reply: "Hello again, nice to be able to see you."

In the early years cows were allowed to roam around the course but now this practice has ceased. The driving force behind its creation was 'Jacko' Jackson and today the club boasts a membership of 250 -300, with no more than a 100 active golfers.

The 412 yard 9th is the longest hole and if you are into useless golf statistics that makes the fairway a quarter of the entire width of Alderney which measures roughly three miles by one when the tide is in. It is also interesting to note, and certainly this was the case when I played there last, that you can hire a golf buggy to drive around the island but it is not permitted to use them on the course? That's not a criticism but another funny fact and makes Alderney that bit different.

ALDERNEY GOLF CLUB